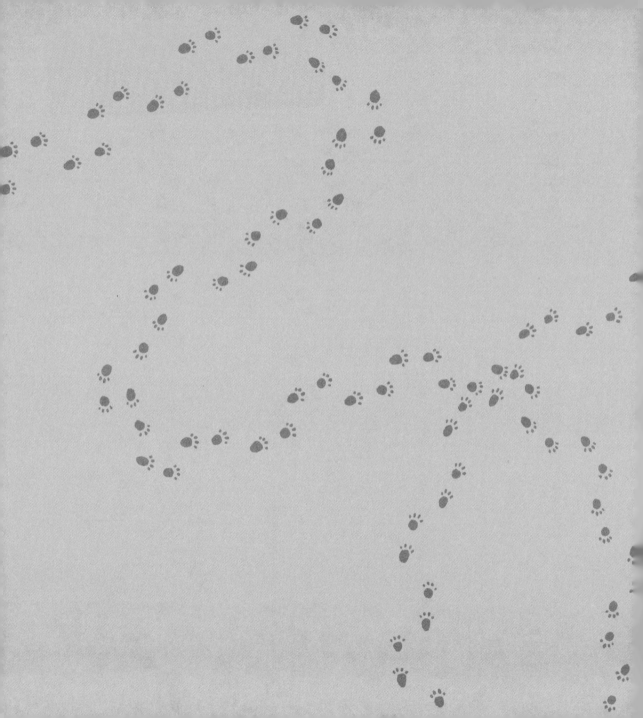

LET'S TALK ABOUT
FEELING WORRIED

by Joy Berry • Illustrated by Maggie Smith

SCHOLASTIC INC.

New York Toronto London Auckland Sydney
Mexico City New Delhi Hong Kong Buenos Aires

Text copyright © 2002 by Joy Berry.
Illustration copyright © 2002 by Scholastic Inc.
All rights reserved. Published by Scholastic Inc., 555 Broadway, New York, NY 10012,
by arrangement with Joy Berry.

No part of this publication may be reproduced in whole or in part, or stored in
a retrieval system, or transmitted in any form or by any means, electronic, mechanical,
photocopying, recording, or otherwise, without written permission
of the author. For information regarding permission, write to Joy Berry,
7540 North Ajo Road, Scottsdale, Arizona 85258.

SCHOLASTIC and associated design is a trademark of Scholastic Inc.

ISBN 0-439-34158-2

10 9 8 7 6 5 4 3 2 1   02 03 04 05 06

Printed in the U.S.A.
First printing, April 2002

Hello, my name is Hammy.

I live with Julia.

Sometimes Julia worries that something might hurt her.

Sometimes Julia worries that she won't be able to do something.

Sometimes Julia worries that others won't like her.

Sometimes Julia worries that she might lose someone or something important to her.

When you feel worried, you might feel anxious, nervous, and upset.

Your body might do strange things when you feel worried.

Your stomach might feel upset.

Your muscles might feel tense.

It might be hard to sleep.

When you feel worried, you might have a hard time thinking about anything else.

When you feel worried, you might imagine all kinds of things.

Most of these things probably won't happen.

Most of these things probably aren't true.

Worrying often keeps you from doing things you want and need to do.

So, try not to spend too much time and energy worrying.

Sometimes it's impossible not to worry.

When this happens, it's best not to ignore your worries.

You can make yourself feel better by talking to someone about what is worrying you.

Describe how you feel.

Ask questions.

Try to learn the facts about what's worrying you.

When you know the facts about something, it's less likely to worry you.

Sometimes you won't be able to stop worrying about something.

When this happens, slow down and relax.

Lie flat on your back and take several deep breaths.

Slowly count to ten.

Sometimes it helps to think fun thoughts or do fun things.

This will help you keep your mind off your worries.

Remember that everyone worries sometimes.

Worrying is okay.

Just try to do things that will make you feel better whenever you feel worried.

Let's talk about... **Joy Berry!**

As the inventor of self-help books for kids, Joy Berry has written over 250 books that teach children about taking responsibility for themselves and their actions. With sales of over 80 million copies, Joy's books have helped millions of parents and their kids.

Through interesting stories that kids can relate to, Joy Berry's Let's Talk About books explain how to handle even the toughest situations and emotions. Written in a clear, simple style and illustrated with bright, humorous pictures, the Let's Talk About books are fun, informative, and they really work!

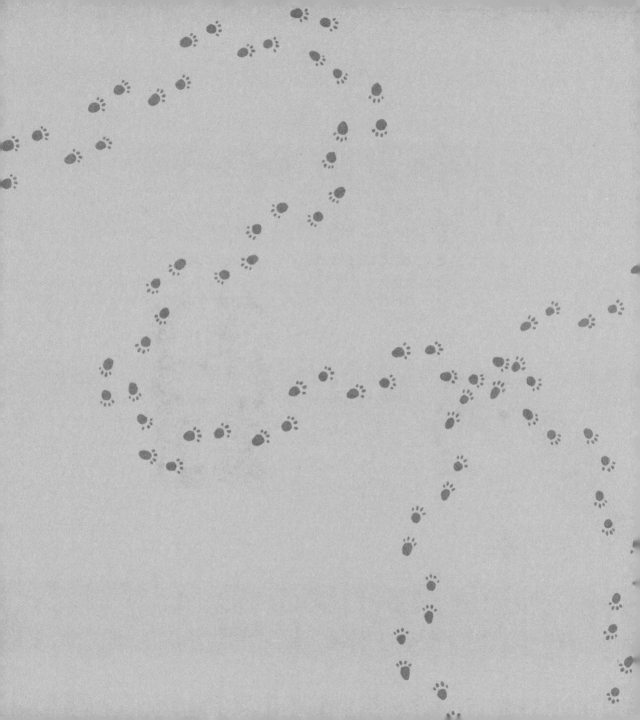